A Journey through Computer and Technology

Aarush Darne

pencil

ISBN 978-93-5883-078-1
© Aarush Darne 2023

Published in India 2023 by Pencil

A brand of
One Point Six Technologies Pvt. Ltd.
Unit no. 26, Ground Floor, Building A1,
Wadala Truck Terminal Road,
Near Post Office, Antop Hill, Mumbai - 400037
E connect@thepencilapp.com
W www.thepencilapp.com

Author biography

My name is Aarush Nishad Darne. I am 12 years old. I study at D.A.V Public School in Navi Mumbai. This is my first book and Pencil writes it. This book contains History and Present about Computers and many other technologies it also contains some predictions about computers and technologies For. Eg- 6G Mobile Network, Wifi 7, XR (Extended Reality). I have also covered topics on cloud storage, big data, green computing, and IT. I have given real-time app examples so you will try it out later. I hope you like my book.

CONTENTS

1. Origins Of Computer

Histroy Of Computers- The origins of computing can be traced back to ancient times when humans used various tools to perform mathematical calculations and solve problems. However, the modern era of computing began in the 19th and 20th centuries with the development of mechanical and electronic devices. Here is an overview of the key milestones in the history of computing:

Abacus (circa 3000 BCE): The abacus, an ancient counting tool, is one of the earliest computing devices. It allowed users to perform basic arithmetic operations by sliding beads along rods.

Mechanical Calculators (17th - 19th centuries): Inventors like Blaise Pascal and Gottfried Wilhelm Leibniz created mechanical calculators in the 17th century, which could perform addition and subtraction through gears and levers. Charles Babbage's designs for the "Analytical Engine" in the 19th century laid the groundwork for modern computing concepts.

Ada Lovelace and the First Computer Program (1843): Ada Lovelace, an English mathematician, wrote the first known algorithm intended to be processed by a machine. She worked with Charles Babbage on the Analytical Engine and is considered the world's first computer programmer.

Tabulating Machines (late 19th - early 20th centuries): Herman Hollerith's tabulating machine, developed in the late 1800s, used punched cards to process and store data. It was used in the 1890 United States Census and later formed the basis for IBM's early machines.

Vacuum Tube Computers (1930s - 1940s): The development of electronic computers began with machines that used vacuum tubes for data processing. One of the earliest electronic computers was the ENIAC (Electronic Numerical Integrator and Computer), completed in 1945, which was used for military calculations during World War II.

Transistors and Integrated Circuits (1950s - 1960s): The invention of transistors and the subsequent development of integrated circuits allowed for the miniaturization of electronic components, making computers smaller, more reliable, and more powerful.

General-Purpose Computers (1950s - 1970s): During this period, computers evolved from specialized machines into general-purpose computers capable of executing various tasks. Pioneering projects like UNIVAC and IBM 360 series contributed to this shift.

The Rise of Personal Computers (1970s - 1980s): The development of microprocessors and the introduction of personal computers by companies like Apple and IBM led to a revolution in computing accessibility.

Internet and World Wide Web (1980s - 1990s): The invention of the Internet and the World Wide Web by Tim Berners-Lee in 1989 transformed computing from isolated systems into a global network of interconnected devices.

Mobile Computing (2000s - present): The widespread adoption of smartphones and tablets brought computing to the hands of billions of people worldwide, leading to a new era of mobile computing and connectivity.

Cloud Computing (2000s - present): Cloud computing emerged, allowing users to access shared computing resources and services over the internet, providing flexibility and scalability for various applications.

The history of computing is marked by numerous breakthroughs and innovations, driven by the efforts of countless inventors, engineers, and visionaries. Today, computing continues to advance rapidly, powering various industries and shaping the way we live, work, and communicate.

2. The Evolution of Hardware

The evolution of hardware refers to the continuous development and improvement of computer and electronic devices over time. It encompasses various technologies, components, and form factors that have evolved to meet the demands of an ever-changing computing landscape. Below, I'll provide a broad overview of the key stagesin the evolution of hardware:The evolution of hardware refers to the continuous development and improvement of computer and electronic devices over time. It encompasses various technologies, components, and form factors that have evolved to meet the demands of an ever-changing computing landscape. Below, I'll provide a broad overview of the key stages in the evolution of hardware:

Early Computing Devices: The history of hardware dates back to the early 19th century when mechanical devices like Charles Babbage's "Analytical Engine" and Ada Lovelace's work laid the theoretical foundations for modern computing. However, it was only in the mid-20th century that electronic computing devices began to take shape.

Vacuum Tubes and Early Computers: In the 1940s, electronic computing machines were built using vacuum tubes, which were large, power-hungry, and prone to frequent failures. Examples of early computers include the Electronic Numerical Integrator and Computer (ENIAC) and the Universal Automatic Computer (UNIVAC).

Transistors: In the late 1940s and early 1950s, transistors were invented, offering a more efficient and reliable alternative to vacuum tubes. Transistors paved the way for miniaturization and faster electronic devices.

Integrated Circuits (ICs): In the 1960s, the development of integrated circuits revolutionized computing technology. Multiple transistors and other components were combined on a single semiconductor chip, leading to significant reductions in size, cost, and power consumption.

Microprocessors and Personal Computers: The 1970s saw the emergence of microprocessors, which are complete central processing units (CPUs) on a single chip. In 1975, the first personal computer, the Altair 8800, was released, marking the beginning of the PC era.

Advancements in Storage: Over the years, various storage technologies have evolved. Magnetic tape and punched cards were early storage media, followed by floppy disks, hard disk drives (HDDs), and eventually solid-state drives (SSDs) and cloud-based storage solutions.

Networking and the Internet: The 1980s and 1990s witnessed the rapid development of networking technologies, leading to the creation of the Internet. This global network revolutionized communication and allowed computers worldwide to connect and share information.

Mobile Devices and Smartphones: In the 2000s, mobile devices, particularly smartphones and tablets, became increasingly popular. These devices integrated powerful processors, touchscreens, and various sensors, enabling a new era of mobile computing and communication.

Advancements in Graphics and GPUs: The demand for better graphics capabilities led to the development of Graphics Processing Units (GPUs), which significantly accelerated graphical processing and contributed to the rise of gaming and other visually-intensive applications.

IoT (Internet of Things) and Wearables: The 2010s saw the rise of the Internet of Things, where everyday objects are connected to the internet, enabling smart homes, wearable devices, and interconnected ecosystems of devices.

Artificial Intelligence and Quantum Computing: In recent years, hardware advancements have been driven by the rise of artificial intelligence and machine learning, leading to specialized AI hardware like GPUs and TPUs (Tensor Processing Units). Quantum computing also emerged as a promising technology, offering the potential for exponentially increased computational power.

The evolution of hardware has been characterized by a continuous push for higher performance, greater efficiency, smaller form factors, and enhanced functionality. These advancements have played a crucial role in shaping the modern world and will continue to drive technological innovation in the future.

3. Software The Soul of the Machine

Introduction In the realm of modern technology, software has emerged as the soul of the machine, breathing life into our devices and empowering them to perform remarkable feats. While hardware provides the physical framework, it is the software that drives the intelligence and functionality of these machines. Just as the soul is to the body, software imbues the machine with consciousness, giving it the ability to interact, process information, and serve as a transformative force in various aspects of human life. This essay explores the significance of software as the driving force behind the machines, its evolution, and its impact on society. The Evolution of Software The journey of software began with simple punch cards and assembly languages, but it has rapidly evolved into complex, dynamic programming languages capable of managing intricate tasks. Early software was primarily used to control calculators and basic automated systems. As technology progressed, so did software, evolving to accommodate diverse applications, including operating systems, business management tools, artistic creations, and scientific simulations. With the advent of personal computers and the internet, software became more accessible, enabling individuals and businesses to harness its power for various purposes. Today, we stand at the forefront of revolutionary advancements like artificial intelligence, machine learning, and quantum computing, where software continues to play a pivotal role in shaping the future. Empowering Technology Software is the catalyst that transforms hardware into a functional and versatile tool. Whether it is our smartphones, laptops, smart home devices, or industrial machinery, it is the software that enables these machines to operate efficiently and serve their intended purposes. The ability to write, modify, and upgrade software allows for continuous improvement and innovation, leading to new and groundbreaking applications across industries. Furthermore, software has extended its influence beyond traditional computing devices. From autonomous vehicles to medical equipment, from space exploration to renewable energy systems, software's reach is vast and continues to expand into uncharted territories. The dynamism and adaptability of software enable machines to perform tasks that were once considered beyond human capabilities, enhancing productivity and efficiency in virtually every field. Solving Complex Problems As software grows in sophistication, it enables the resolution of complex problems that would be impossible to tackle manually. Data analysis and machine learning algorithms can process vast amounts of information in real-time, leading to insights that drive decision-making in various sectors, including finance, healthcare, and environmental science. In addition, software simulations play a crucial role in research and development, allowing scientists and engineers to model complex systems, test hypotheses, and optimize designs before investing substantial resources into physical prototypes. This iterative process has accelerated progress in countless industries, saving time and resources while enhancing the quality of final products. Impact on Society The influence of software on society cannot be understated. It has revolutionized communication, bringing people from different corners of the world closer together. Social media platforms, messaging apps, and video conferencing software have transformed the way we connect, share information, and collaborate on a global scale. Moreover, software has democratized education, making learning accessible to millions through online courses, virtual classrooms, and interactive learning platforms. It has also revolutionized healthcare by powering telemedicine, medical imaging, and diagnostic tools, enhancing patient care and reducing geographical barriers to medical expertise. However, the growing reliance on software has also raised concerns about security and privacy. The interconnectedness of systems and data makes them vulnerable to cyberattacks and data breaches. Consequently, ensuring the safety and integrity of software has become a critical challenge that requires ongoing vigilance and robust cybersecurity measures. Conclusion Software, as the soul of the machine, continues to shape our lives in profound ways. From powering our everyday gadgets to revolutionizing industries and connecting people worldwide, software is the driving force behind technological progress. Its evolution has been marked by unprecedented advancements, enabling us to tackle complex problems and make the impossible possible. As we move forward, embracing software's potential while addressing its challenges will be crucial in ensuring a bright and transformative future for humanity

4. Networking and Communication Connecting the World

Introduction: In the modern age, the world has become increasingly interconnected through networking and communication technologies. The rapid advancements in information technology have revolutionized the way we interact, share information, and conduct business. Networking and communication play a pivotal role in facilitating the exchange of data, ideas, and knowledge across the globe. This essay explores the significance of networking and communication in shaping today's interconnected world.

The Evolution of Networking:

The concept of networking dates back to the early days of communication when humans used smoke signals, drums, and carrier pigeons to convey messages across distances. Over time, the development of the telegraph, telephone, and radio marked significant milestones in communication technology. However, the true revolution came with the advent of the Internet in the late 20th century. The Internet connected people and devices, opening up vast opportunities for data exchange and collaboration.

The Power of the Internet:

The Internet has become the backbone of modern networking and communication. It has transformed the way we live, work, and interact. Through the Internet, people can connect with each other instantly, irrespective of their geographic locations. Social media platforms, emails, and video conferencing applications have become essential tools for personal and professional communication. Moreover, the Internet has fostered globalization, enabling businesses to operate internationally and reach a broader customer base. E-commerce has boomed, providing consumers with access to products and services from around the world. This interconnectedness has strengthened international cooperation and cultural exchange, promoting understanding and empathy among diverse communities.

Networking in the Business World:

Networking has revolutionized the business landscape, enabling enterprises to streamline operations and increase efficiency. Local area networks (LANs) and wide area networks (WANs) have become standard in offices, facilitating real-time data sharing and collaboration among employees. Cloud computing has further enhanced the accessibility and storage of vast amounts of data, allowing businesses to scale and adapt swiftly. Additionally, the rise of the Internet of Things (IoT) has expanded networking beyond computers and smartphones. IoT devices, such as smart sensors, wearables, and home automation systems, communicate with each other, generating valuable data for businesses and improving the quality of life for individuals.

Communication and Social Interaction:

Communication has always been an integral part of human society. In the digital era, the ways we communicate have undergone a significant transformation. Instant messaging, social media, and video calls have become the norm for interpersonal interactions. While these technologies offer convenience, they also come with challenges, such as privacy concerns and the potential for misinformation spread. However, the benefits of improved communication cannot be overlooked. The ability to connect with friends, family, and colleagues from anywhere in the world fosters stronger relationships and promotes collaboration on a global scale. It has also empowered individuals to raise their voices and advocate for social causes, leading to positive changes in societies worldwide.

Networking and Communication Challenges:

Despite the numerous advantages of networking and communication, there are challenges that need to be addressed. Cybersecurity threats, such as hacking, data breaches, and phishing, pose significant risks to individuals and organizations. Strengthening cybersecurity measures is crucial to protect sensitive data and ensure safe communication channels. Additionally, the digital divide remains a considerable obstacle in achieving global connectivity. Many regions, especially in developing countries, lack access to reliable internet infrastructure, hindering their ability to fully participate in the digital world. Bridging this gap requires collaborative efforts between governments, private sector companies, and international organizations. Conclusion: Networking and communication have transformed the world into a tightly-knit global community. The Internet, along with various networking technologies, has revolutionized the way we interact, do business, and share knowledge. The ease of communication has brought people together, transcending geographical boundaries and fostering a greater understanding of diverse cultures and perspectives. As we move forward, it is vital to address the challenges posed by networking and communication, such as cybersecurity and the digital divide. By doing so, we can ensure that the benefits of connectivity and information exchange are accessible to all, contributing to a more inclusive and prosperous world.

5. Artificial Intelligence and Machine Learning

Artificial Intelligence (AI) and Machine Learning (ML) are two closely related fields that have garnered significant attention and advancements in recent years. They both aim to create systems that can perform tasks that typically require human intelligence. However, they differ in their approaches and applications. Artificial Intelligence (AI): AI is a broad concept that refers to the development of computer systems capable of simulating human-like intelligence. The goal of AI is to enable machines to perceive, reason, learn from experience, and make decisions in a way that mimics human cognitive abilities. AI can be classified into two main categories:

Narrow AI (Weak AI): This refers to AI systems designed to perform specific tasks or solve particular problems. Examples include virtual personal assistants like Siri and Alexa, recommendation algorithms on streaming platforms, and fraud detection systems in banking.
General AI (Strong AI): This is the hypothetical AI system that possesses human-level intelligence and can perform any intellectual task that a human can do. Creating a true general AI remains a significant challenge and is an ongoing topic of research.

Machine Learning (ML): Machine Learning is a subset of AI and is a specific approach to achieve AI's goals. It focuses on developing algorithms that can learn patterns and make predictions from data without being explicitly programmed for each task. The learning process in ML involves using statistical techniques to enable the system to improve its performance on a specific task over time. Types of Machine Learning:

Supervised Learning: The algorithm is trained on labeled data, where the correct output is provided, and the goal is to make predictions on new, unseen data.

Unsupervised Learning: The algorithm is trained on unlabeled data and tries to find patterns and structures in the data without explicit guidance.

Semi-supervised Learning: This approach uses a combination of labeled and unlabeled data for training.

Reinforcement Learning: The algorithm learns through a system of rewards and punishments, interacting with an environment to achieve specific goals.

Applications of AI and Machine Learning: AI and ML have found applications in various industries and domains, including:

Healthcare: Diagnosis, drug discovery, personalized medicine, and medical image analysis.

Finance: Fraud detection, algorithmic trading, credit risk assessment, and customer service.

Transportation: Autonomous vehicles, route optimization, and traffic management.

Natural Language Processing (NLP): Sentiment analysis, language translation, chatbots, and voice assistants.

Robotics: Industrial automation, drones, and social robots.
Gaming: Intelligent opponents and procedural content generation.
Marketing and Sales: Customer segmentation, targeted advertising, and demand prediction.
Recommender Systems: Content recommendation on streaming platforms and e-commerce websites.

The field of AI and Machine Learning is continuously evolving, and researchers and developers are making strides to create more sophisticated, ethical, and beneficial applications of these technologies to improve various aspects of our lives.

6. The Internet of Things (IoT) Revolutionizing the Connected World

Introduction: The Internet of Things (IoT) has emerged as one of the most transformative and innovative technologies of the 21st century. It represents a vast network of interconnected devices and objects, enabling them to collect, exchange, and act upon data, all while seamlessly integrating with our daily lives. IoT has the potential to revolutionize industries, enhance efficiency, and provide novel solutions to complex problems. This essay delves into the concept, applications, challenges, and future prospects of the Internet of Things. Understanding the Internet of Things (IoT): At its core, the Internet of Things refers to the interconnection of physical devices, vehicles, appliances, and even buildings, embedded with sensors, software, and connectivity, allowing them to collect and exchange data. These devices communicate with each other through the internet or other networks, thereby creating an ecosystem of smart, responsive, and interconnected objects. IoT technology empowers these devices to collect real-time data, analyze it, and take appropriate actions autonomously or with human intervention. Applications of IoT:

Smart Homes: IoT has revolutionized the concept of smart homes, allowing homeowners to control and monitor appliances, lighting, heating, and security systems remotely. It enhances convenience, energy efficiency, and security.

Healthcare: In the healthcare sector, IoT enables remote patient monitoring, wearable health devices, and smart medical equipment. It enhances patient care, enables early detection of health issues, and reduces hospitalization.

Transportation and Logistics: IoT plays a crucial role in fleet management, logistics optimization, and autonomous vehicles. It improves transportation efficiency, safety, and reduces fuel consumption.

Agriculture: IoT-powered sensors and devices help farmers monitor soil conditions, weather patterns, and livestock health, leading to precision agriculture and increased yields.

Industrial IoT (IIoT): In the manufacturing sector, IIoT enhances operational efficiency, predictive maintenance, and overall production through real-time monitoring of machines and processes.

Smart Cities: IoT contributes to building smarter and more sustainable cities by optimizing waste management, traffic control, energy consumption, and public services.

Challenges and Concerns:

Security and Privacy: With billions of devices interconnected, security vulnerabilities become a significant concern. Unauthorized access to sensitive data or manipulation of connected devices poses risks to individuals and organizations.

Interoperability: The lack of standardized protocols and communication interfaces can hinder seamless interoperability between different IoT devices and platforms.

Data Overload: The massive volume of data generated by IoT devices can overwhelm systems and networks, making data processing and analysis challenging.

Reliability and Downtime: The dependence on constant connectivity makes IoT susceptible to network failures, leading to downtime and potential disruptions.

Ethical Considerations: The widespread adoption of IoT raises ethical questions concerning data ownership, consent, and the potential misuse of personal information.

The Future of IoT: The Internet of Things is continually evolving and is expected to have a profound impact on various aspects of society in the future. Several trends are shaping the future of IoT:

5G Connectivity: The rollout of 5G networks will provide faster and more reliable connectivity, essential for supporting a massive number of IoT devices.

Edge Computing: Moving data processing and analysis closer to the source (at the edge) will reduce latency, enhance real-time decision-making, and alleviate the strain on cloud infrastructure.

AI and Machine Learning Integration: IoT devices will become smarter with the integration of artificial intelligence and machine learning algorithms, enabling them to learn from data and make more informed decisions.

Blockchain Integration: Blockchain technology will enhance the security and privacy aspects of IoT, ensuring tamper-resistant data storage and transparent data sharing.

Environmental Sustainability: IoT can contribute to environmental sustainability by enabling smarter resource management and reducing energy consumption in various sectors.

Conclusion: The Internet of Things has already proven to be a game-changer, revolutionizing the way we interact with technology and the world around us. Its potential applications are vast, and as technology continues to evolve, IoT will become even more integral to our lives. However, along with the opportunities, there are challenges to be addressed, such as security, privacy, and ethical concerns. It is crucial for governments, industries, and individuals to collaborate in creating a robust and secure IoT ecosystem that maximizes the benefits while minimizing the risks. By doing so, we can harness the full potential of IoT and usher in a new era of connectivity and innovation.

7. Cloud Computing and Big Data

Cloud Computing: Cloud computing is a paradigm that enables access to a shared pool of computing resources (such as servers, storage, databases, networking, software, and more) over the internet. Instead of relying on local servers or infrastructure, cloud computing allows users to leverage remote data centers maintained by third-party providers. Key features of cloud computing include:

On-Demand Self-Service: Users can provision and manage resources independently without direct interaction with the cloud service provider.

Broad Network Access: Cloud services are accessible over the internet from a wide range of devices, such as computers, smartphones, and tablets.

Resource Pooling: Computing resources are pooled and shared among multiple users, allowing for more efficient utilization and scalability.

Rapid Elasticity: Users can quickly scale resources up or down based on their needs, often in an automated manner, which helps handle varying workloads efficiently.

Measured Service: Cloud computing resources are typically metered, and users pay only for the resources they consume, promoting cost-efficiency.

Cloud computing offers various deployment models, including Public Cloud, Private Cloud, Hybrid Cloud, and Community Cloud. Popular cloud service providers include Amazon Web Services (AWS), Microsoft Azure, Google Cloud Platform (GCP), and others. Big Data: Big data refers to extremely large and complex datasets that cannot be effectively processed using traditional data processing applications. The term "big data" encompasses the volume, velocity, and variety of data. The three main characteristics are:

Volume: The sheer size of the data generated, which can range from terabytes to petabytes and beyond.
Velocity: The speed at which data is generated and collected, often in real-time or near real-time.
Variety: The diverse types of data, including structured, semi-structured, and unstructured data, such as text, images, videos, social media interactions, sensor data, etc.

Big data is valuable because it contains insights and patterns that, when analyzed, can lead to better decision-making, improved operational efficiency, and enhanced customer experiences. However, traditional databases and data processing techniques are inadequate for handling big data due to its scale and complexity. The Intersection of Cloud Computing and Big Data: Cloud computing plays a crucial role in the big data ecosystem for several reasons:

Scalability: Cloud providers offer scalable infrastructure that can handle large volumes of data and processing demands, allowing organizations to adjust resources as needed.

Cost-Efficiency: Instead of investing in expensive on-premises infrastructure, organizations can use the pay-as-you-go model of cloud computing, reducing capital expenses.

Accessibility: Cloud-based big data platforms enable distributed access to data and analytics tools, making collaboration easier for geographically dispersed teams.

Flexibility: Cloud platforms support a wide array of big data technologies and frameworks, such as Apache Hadoop, Apache Spark, and various NoSQL databases.

Data Processing Power: Cloud providers offer powerful processing capabilities, enabling faster and more efficient data analysis.

Security and Compliance: Reputable cloud service providers implement robust security measures, which is especially crucial when dealing with sensitive big data.

In conclusion, cloud computing and big data are complementary technologies that have revolutionized the way organizations store, manage, and derive insights from massive amounts of data. The combination of these technologies empowers businesses to harness the potential of big data while enjoying the flexibility, scalability, and cost-efficiency provided by cloud computing services.

8. Virtual and Augmented Reality

Virtual Reality (VR) and Augmented Reality (AR) are two distinct technologies that aim to enhance our sensory experiences and interactions with the digital world. They both have the common goal of creating immersive experiences, but they do so in different ways and serve different purposes.

Virtual Reality (VR): Virtual Reality refers to a computer-generated simulation or environment that immerses users into a completely synthetic, three-dimensional world. VR typically involves wearing a head-mounted display (HMD) or goggles that cover the user's eyes, shutting out the physical world and replacing it with a digital, virtual one. VR systems often include motion tracking technology to detect the user's movements and adjust the virtual environment accordingly, creating a sense of presence and realism.

Applications of Virtual Reality:

Gaming and Entertainment: VR is widely used in gaming to provide players with a more immersive and realistic gaming experience. Training and Simulation: VR is utilized for various training scenarios, such as flight simulations, medical training, military drills, and industrial training. Education: VR is being integrated into educational settings to make learning more engaging and interactive. Therapy and Rehabilitation: VR is used in healthcare to aid in therapy and rehabilitation for certain medical conditions. Augmented Reality (AR): Augmented Reality involves overlaying digital content or information onto the real-world environment, thus enhancing the user's perception of reality. Unlike VR, AR does not replace the real world entirely; instead, it supplements it with computer-generated elements that interact with the physical environment in real-time. AR can be experienced through various devices, such as smartphones, tablets, smart glasses, and AR headsets.

Applications of Augmented Reality:

Mobile Apps: AR is commonly integrated into mobile applications to provide users with enhanced experiences, such as interactive product demonstrations or location-based information. Navigation: AR navigation systems can overlay directions and points of interest on the real world as users move through their environment. Retail: AR is used in retail to enable customers to visualize products in their real-world surroundings before making a purchase. Industrial and Maintenance: AR is applied in industries to provide workers with real-time data and instructions, making tasks more efficient and error-free.

It's worth noting that the lines between VR and AR are sometimes blurred, and some devices and applications can incorporate both technologies, known as Mixed Reality (MR). Mixed Reality allows digital objects to interact with and respond to the real world, providing users with a more seamless and immersive experience. Both VR and AR have seen significant advancements in recent years, and their potential applications continue to expand, revolutionizing various industries and aspects of our lives.

9. Green Computing and Sustainability

Green computing, also known as green IT or sustainable computing, refers to the practice of designing, using, and managing computer systems and technology in an environmentally responsible and energy-efficient manner. The goal of green computing is to reduce the environmental impact of information technology while promoting sustainability and efficiency. Key aspects of green computing and sustainability include:

Energy Efficiency: One of the primary focuses of green computing is to reduce energy consumption. This can be achieved through various means, such as using energy-efficient hardware components, optimizing software to consume less power, and employing power management techniques like sleep mode and dynamic frequency scaling.

Renewable Energy: Utilizing renewable energy sources to power data centers and computing infrastructure is an essential step towards sustainability. Solar, wind, hydroelectric, and other clean energy sources can help reduce the carbon footprint of IT operations.

E-waste Management: With the rapid advancement of technology, electronic waste (e-waste) has become a significant concern. Green computing emphasizes responsible recycling and disposal of old or obsolete electronic equipment to prevent environmental contamination.

Virtualization and Cloud Computing: Virtualization allows multiple virtual machines to run on a single physical machine, reducing the overall hardware requirements and increasing resource utilization. Cloud computing also enables better resource allocation, leading to energy and cost savings.

Sustainable Materials: Manufacturers are encouraged to use environmentally friendly and recyclable materials in the production of computer hardware to reduce the environmental impact of the entire lifecycle of the product.

Green Data Centers: Data centers are major consumers of electricity, and efforts are made to design and operate them in an energy-efficient manner. This includes using advanced cooling techniques, optimizing server placement, and maximizing server utilization.

Green Software Development: Software developers play a vital role in green computing by writing code that is optimized for energy efficiency, reducing resource usage, and adopting eco-friendly programming practices.

Telecommuting and Remote Work: Encouraging telecommuting and remote work can reduce the need for daily commuting, resulting in lower carbon emissions and energy usage.

Education and Awareness: Promoting awareness and educating users, businesses, and organizations about the importance of green computing practices is crucial in driving sustainable change.

The adoption of green computing practices not only benefits the environment by reducing greenhouse gas emissions and resource consumption but also helps organizations save on operational costs in the long run. It is a collective effort that involves individuals, businesses, governments, and the technology industry to work together towards a more sustainable future.

33

10. The Future of Computing and Technology

Quantum Computing: Quantum computing holds great promise for solving complex problems that are practically impossible for classical computers. As technology advances, we may witness more practical quantum computers, which could revolutionize fields like cryptography, drug discovery, optimization, and material science.

AI and Machine Learning: Artificial Intelligence (AI) and Machine Learning (ML) will continue to permeate various industries and become more integrated into everyday life. Autonomous systems, natural language processing, computer vision, and AI-driven decision-making are likely to see significant progress.

5G and Beyond: The rollout and optimization of 5G networks will pave the way for enhanced mobile connectivity and faster data transmission. Beyond 5G, technologies like 6G or even more advanced wireless networks might emerge, enabling new applications and services.

Internet of Things (IoT): IoT will become more prevalent, with an increasing number of connected devices in homes, cities, industries, and agriculture. The seamless integration of IoT into various sectors will lead to improved efficiency and convenience.

Extended Reality (XR): Extended Reality, which includes Virtual Reality (VR), Augmented Reality (AR), and Mixed Reality (MR), is poised to transform entertainment, education, training, and communication, offering immersive and interactive experiences.

Edge Computing: With the growing amount of data generated by IoT devices and AI applications, there will be a greater emphasis on edge computing. Processing data closer to the source, rather than sending it to centralized servers, will reduce latency and bandwidth demands.

Biotechnology and Healthcare: Advancements in technology will continue to shape the field of healthcare and biotechnology. Personalized medicine, gene editing, and wearable health devices are some areas to watch for significant breakthroughs.

Robotics and Automation: Robotics and automation will find broader applications in various industries, from manufacturing and logistics to healthcare and agriculture, leading to increased efficiency and productivity.

Green Technology: Concerns about climate change will drive innovation in green technology. Expect to see developments in renewable energy, energy storage, sustainable materials, and environmentally friendly practices in the tech sector.

Cybersecurity: As technology advances, so will cyber threats. The future will see increased focus on developing robust cybersecurity measures to safeguard data, infrastructure, and privacy.

Ethics and Regulation: The rapid pace of technological development will necessitate ongoing discussions about ethical considerations and the need for appropriate regulations to ensure responsible use of technology.

Space Exploration and Colonization: Advancements in space technology may lead to increased exploration of space, including missions to other planets and the establishment of human colonies on celestial bodies like the Moon or Mars.

Conclusion

In Conclusion- The journey of computer and technology has been nothing short of remarkable. From the humble beginnings of mechanical calculators and punch cards to the sophisticated world of artificial intelligence and quantum computing, the evolution of technology has shaped and reshaped our world in ways that were once unimaginable. Looking back on this incredible journey, we can marvel at the ingenuity, perseverance, and curiosity of human beings that have driven these advancements. Throughout history, computers and technology have transformed every aspect of our lives. They have revolutionized communication, education, healthcare, transportation, and virtually every other industry. The digital age has interconnected people across the globe, breaking down barriers and fostering an unprecedented exchange of ideas and information. The democratization of knowledge has empowered individuals, while new forms of art, entertainment, and creativity have emerged, enriching our cultural landscape. However, this journey has not been without its challenges. Alongside the tremendous benefits, there have been concerns about the impact of technology on privacy, cybersecurity, and social dynamics. As we continue to embrace the future, it is crucial to approach it with a sense of responsibility. We must be mindful of how technology is affecting our society, taking proactive steps to address its negative consequences and ensuring that it serves the greater good. Moreover, embracing the future also demands innovation. We must not rest on past achievements but push forward with fresh ideas and novel approaches. The rapid pace of technological change requires continuous adaptation and improvement. By encouraging research, fostering a culture of creativity, and supporting entrepreneurship, we can create an environment where innovation thrives. In this process, it is vital to consider the ethical implications of new technologies. Ethical standards and guidelines should be at the core of every technological development. We must prioritize the well-being of individuals and communities, avoiding the exploitation of technology for harmful purposes. A transparent and inclusive approach will enable us to create technologies that truly benefit everyone. As we reflect on the journey of computer and technology, we recognize that we stand at a critical juncture. The future holds immense possibilities, from advancements in artificial intelligence and robotics to space exploration and sustainable technologies. It is up to us, as a global community, to navigate this future with wisdom, empathy, and a commitment to progress. Embracing the future with responsibility and innovation means envisioning a world where technology is harnessed to address pressing challenges such as climate change, poverty, and inequality. It involves using technology to improve healthcare outcomes, enhance education, and create meaningful employment opportunities. By leveraging the power of technology responsibly, we can build a more equitable and sustainable future for all. In conclusion, the journey of computer and technology has been awe-inspiring, and we owe it to ourselves and future generations to continue this path with responsibility and innovation. By reflecting on the past, learning from our experiences, and embracing a future that prioritizes ethical considerations and pushes the boundaries of human ingenuity, we can shape a world that is both advanced and compassionate. Let us move forward together, united by a common vision of a brighter future for humanity.